My Ladybug Garden Coloring Book

Illustrations by Mrs. Lynnette Jones

DEDICATION
For my husband and my daughters.
I Love You!

Copyright © 2017 Mrs. Lynnette Ewoldt Jones   www.MyArtByLynnette.biz
All rights reserved.

ISBN:
ISBN-13: 9781548376819

ISBN-10: 1548376817

Give the *Gift* of *Kindness* to Everyone you meet!

www.MyArtByLynnette.biz

Spot

New

Opportunities

Dream it,

Wish it,

DO IT!

The Nature of Life is to Grow in Happiness!

Appreciate the *Little Things*

Lovely little Ladybug

Sent from

Heaven above

Watch over my home

And fill it with

Love!

Polka dots and little black spots that's what ladybugs are made of.

Throw Happiness Around like Confetti

Ladybugs

Are Bundles

Of

Bliss!

She Designed

The Life

She Lived

www.MyArtByLynnette.biz

BIG
Things often have
Small
Beginnings!

I Love You

More!

They claim to be Bugs, but they are really Beetles

www.MyArtByLynnette.biz

Ladybugs are Lucky

And I know I am lucky too

since I have a good friend like you.

www.MyArtByLynnette.biz

Positive Thinking, POSITIVE OUTCOME

You will never be lost

following

your DREAMS

YOU GOT THIS!

www.MyArtByLynnette.biz

Don't let the
Small things

Bug you!

Stop Dreaming.

Start

Doing!

Ladybug rules:

Always eat like a Lady

Be well Rounded

and Show your

True Colors!

www.MyArtByLynnette.biz

BE CALM & BUZZ ON

Life doesn't have to be perfect to be Wonderful!

Don't wait for someone to give you *Flowers,* Plant your own Garden and *Decorate your Soul*

Whisper *I Love You* to a Ladybug and she will fly off to deliver your message.

Great things never Come from Comfort Zones

Made in the USA
Coppell, TX
27 April 2020